LIFE STORY
BEAR

MIKE DOWN

Illustrated by
David McAllister

Troll Associates

Library of Congress Cataloging-in-Publication Data

Down, Mike, (date)
    Bear / by Mike Down ; illustrated by David McAllister.
        p.   cm. — (Life story)
    Summary: Describes the physical characteristics, habits, and life
cycle of the brown bear.
    ISBN 0-8167-2765-1 (lib. bdg.)   ISBN 0-8167-2766-X (pbk.)
    I. Brown bear—Juvenile literature.   2. Bears—Juvenile
literature.   [1. Brown bears.   2. Bears.]   I. McAllister, David,
ill.   II. Title.   III. Series.
QL737.C27D68 1993
599.74'446—dc20   91-44726

Published by Troll Associates

© 1994 Eagle Books

This edition published in 2003.

Design by James Marks
Edited by Kate Woodhouse
Picture research by Jan Croot

Printed in U.S.A.

10 9 8 7 6 5 4

Photographs by:
Andrea/Jean-Paul Ferrero: 7, 9, 11, 21
Andrea/François Gehier: 5
FLPA/Mark Newman: 15, 19
NHPA/Henry Ansloos: 17
NHPA/Stephen J. Krasemann: 29
NHPA/John Shaw: 25
NHPA/Harry Teyu: 23
Survival Anglia/Joel Bennett: cover
ZEFA/T. Walker: 27
ZEFA/Art Wolfe: 13

INTRODUCTION

Bears are large, strong, meat-eating mammals that live in some of the remotest places on Earth.

In this book we follow the life of brown bears through the four seasons. In spring they emerge sleepy and hungry from their dens. In summer they mate, then feed on fish from the river.

In autumn they gorge on berries and put on weight. In winter, while sleeping in their dens beneath the snow, they give birth to their cubs.

These wonderful creatures have lived on Earth in their present form for over a million years, and this is your chance to discover more about them.

Brown bears are the world's mightiest meat eaters. They have no natural enemies except people, and they eat almost everything. They live in remote forests and mountains in North America, northern Russia, and a few other parts of Europe and Asia.

The brown bear in the photograph lives on the coast of Alaska. It stands 8 feet (almost 2.5 meters) tall on its back legs, and weighs as much as a car. It can charge at about 30 miles per hour (50 kilometers per hour). Its jaws can slice bones as if they were matchsticks.

When spring comes, bears are hungry after their winter sleep. They will search for grass and other plants beneath the melting snow.

Like other mammals, brown bears are warm-blooded and have hair on their bodies. They live in colder places than most other mammals, and need two coats. The topcoat is made of long rough hairs, which guard the bear from bad weather. The fleecy undercoat keeps them warm.

As the days get warmer, bears start to molt. The old hairs fall out and are replaced by shorter, less dense, hairs.

This bear is dark brown, but there are brown bears of every shade, from cream to almost black.

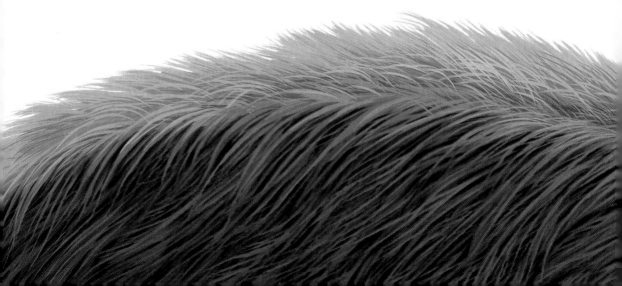

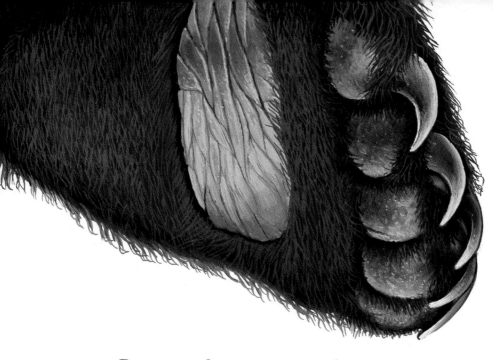

Bears are fast movers and can outrun a horse. They never walk on tiptoe like dogs and cats. A bear's feet are about the same length as an adult human's, but twice as wide.

Each foot has five curved claws. The front claws are long and very sharp—up to 5 inches (12 centimeters)—but wear down during the year. They are used for digging and slashing.

Brown bears use familiar trails to favorite feeding places. These trails get deeper and bumpier over the years. When brown bears gallop, they leave behind a track of footprints 10 feet (3 meters) apart.

Bears are carnivores and prefer meat, but they will also eat plants.

Brown bears sniff out mice, squirrels, fish, ants, and other small animals. They seldom hunt deer, moose, seals, and bison, but they will try to catch any that are old, sick, or very young. They also eat any dead animals that they find, sometimes sharing them with wolves.

Brown bears love honey and rip open tree trunks to get at bees' nests. A bee sting cannot reach through a bear's fur.

But these foods are luxuries. A brown bear usually eats its way through a huge pile of moss, grass, bulbs, berries, nuts, and mushrooms every day.

Bears live alone in their own home area. They mark its borders by scratching and rubbing against trees. When a bear's neighbors see and smell these marks, they keep away.

Male bears have larger home areas, which overlap with the females', but they seldom meet except in the breeding season. When bears meet, they challenge each other. The bigger one stretches out its head and bares its teeth, making the smaller bear turn and slink away. If they are equally matched, they may fight to the death.

Brown bears breed in early summer. A male bear sniffs out the female and starts to feed close by. They challenge each other at first, but after a few weeks they become more content and mate. Several eggs are fertilized inside the female, but they do not start to grow for another six months. The male soon wanders off. He will never see his cubs.

Female bears start breeding between four and eight years old and stop at about fifteen. They mate only a few times in their lives.

In summer, fat, juicy salmon swim from the seas to breed in the inland rivers where they were born. In Alaska, brown bears from far and wide move down to the rivers to feed. They squabble over the best fishing places.

Young bears and females with cubs have to wait until the others have finished. Big males sometimes kill smaller bears that get in their way.

The bears crash through the water, pinning down the wriggling fish with their claws. Sometimes they catch them directly in their jaws. The bears gorge for weeks, and put on weight to help them through the coming winter.

When autumn comes the days start to grow colder. The bears go back to the hills, eating fruit, berries, and nuts along the way. They claw down branches with their paws. They stretch their necks and bite off branches, and stand on their back legs to reach higher. If the bear cannot reach the fruit, it just leans against the tree and pushes it over.

By the time winter arrives, the brown bears have a 5-inch (12-centimeter) layer of fat under their skin.

When the winter snow begins to fall it gets bitterly cold. Many animals move to warmer places where they can still find food, but brown bears survive by going to sleep.

The bears start to dig their dens. This bear is digging hers in the side of a hill. She then carpets it with leaves. Other brown bears den in caves and tree trunks. Some male bears living in places with mild winters do not den at all.

Inside her den, the bear falls into a deep sleep. Some scientists think that while the bear sleeps, her heart beats at half its usual rate and her breathing is shallow, but she stays warm.

These cubs were born in the middle of winter, in a den deep beneath the snow. The cubs begin to grow inside their mother at the start of winter. They are born blind, deaf, toothless, and almost hairless.

Inside the den the cubs feed on their mother's milk. They grow quickly. When they are born, they weigh about one pound (454 grams), but four months later they weigh about 7 pounds (over 3 kilograms). Their mother loses about a quarter of her weight keeping herself warm and producing milk. Mother and cubs come out of the den in spring.

By now the cubs are four months old
and have grown a thick fur coat. They
look at their new surroundings with
bright eyes. They are ready to eat solid
food as well as their mother's milk.

The mother shows her cubs how to
find food and protects them from
danger. They are playful, and like
chasing birds and climbing trees.

They all spend one more winter
together, in a new den. Then, when
they are between one and a half and
three years old, the cubs wander off to
lead their own lives.

There are fewer brown bears alive today than at any time in the past million years. Brown bears need lots of space, but people are using more and more of this space to build farms and houses. Bears breed very slowly and have few cubs, so the death of even one bear takes years to make up.

Grizzlies, like the bear in the photograph, once ranged from Alaska to Mexico. Now these mighty bears have almost disappeared south of Canada. Experts say that bears can only be saved from extinction by controlling hunting, and by conserving the rivers and forests where they live.

Asian black bear

sun bear

There are six types of bears besides brown bears. Polar bears live in the Arctic. They make their dens in the ice. Black bears live in America. Both are very much like brown bears.

Sloth bears live in India and Sri Lanka and mainly come out at night. They use their long snouts to suck up their food. Sun bears are the smallest bears. They are found in southeast Asia and look like dogs with long claws.

Asian black bears nest in trees. Spectacled bears are the only bears south of the equator. They live in the high forests and mountains of South America.

Like the brown bear, these bears are struggling to survive. We must do all we can to help these magnificent animals.

sloth bear

spectacled bear

Fascinating facts

The brown bear's closest relative is the polar bear. The two share an ancestor that lived in Asia about 70,000 years ago.

Brown bears entered America from Asia about 50,000 years ago, when the sea was lower and the two continents were joined.

Brown bears have smaller babies for their adult size than any other mammal except marsupials. It would take hundreds of cubs to weigh as much as a full-grown bear!

By using radio collars, which transmit signals to satellites overhead, scientists can track

bears. They have found that big males have home areas covering 1,500 square miles (3,900 square kilometers). However, the size of the home area of bears varies greatly. Grizzlies in Alaska and Alberta in Canada have a smaller range than those in the colder Northwest Territories of Canada. Some grizzlies may have a range of only 10–12 square miles (30 square kilometers).

Bears' nearest relatives are pandas, raccoons, and dogs. The other families of carnivores, such as cats, weasels, and mongooses, are only distantly related to the bear family.

Giant pandas look like bears, but they are more closely related to raccoons. Koala "bears" are neither bears nor carnivores, although they are mammals. Koalas are related to kangaroos.

The largest known brown bear was discovered in Alaska in 1894. His skin was 13 feet (4 meters) long from nose to tail. The heaviest brown bear lived in Cheyenne Mountain Zoological Park, Colorado, USA, and weighed 1,670 pounds (760 kilograms). The oldest lived to the age of 47.

Some brown bears gather at picnic places, campsites, and farms. When people disturb them, they sometimes attack. Mothers with cubs and old males are particularly dangerous. Experts say the best thing to do if attacked is to lie down and pretend you are dead.

Index

Asian black bears, 28
attacking, 31

birth, 3, 22
black bears, 28
breathing, 20
breeding, 3, 12, 14, 26

carnivores, 10, 31
cats, 8, 31
challenging, 12, 14
charging, 4
claws, 8, 16, 18, 28
cubs, 3, 14, 16, 22, 24, 26, 28,
    30–31

death, 12, 26, 31
dens, 3, 20, 22, 24, 28
digging, 8, 20
dogs, 8, 28, 31

feeding, 3, 8, 14, 16, 22
feet, 8, 18
females, 12, 14, 16, 20, 31
fighting, 12
food, 3, 6, 10, 16, 18, 20, 24,
    28
forests, 4, 26, 28
fur, 6, 10, 22, 24

giant pandas, 31
grizzly bears, 26, 31

hair. See fur
height, 4
hills, 18, 20
home areas, 12, 31
hunting, 10, 26

jaws, 4, 16

koalas, 31

males, 12, 14, 16, 20, 31
mammals, 3, 6, 30–31
marsupials, 30
mating. See breeding
meat, 3–4, 10
milk, 22, 24
molting, 6
mongooses, 31
mountains, 4, 28
movement, 8

number of bears, 26

pandas. See giant panda
plants, 6, 10
play, 24
polar bears, 28, 30
protection of cubs, 24

raccoons, 31
radio collars, 30
rivers, 3, 16, 26

salmon, 16
size, 4, 22, 28, 31
skin, 18, 31
sleeping, 3, 6, 20
sloth bears, 28
spectacled bears, 28
speed, 4, 8
squirrels, 10
sun bears, 28
survival, 26, 28

teeth, 12
trails, 8
trees, 10, 12, 18, 20, 24, 28

weasels, 31
weight, 3, 4, 16, 22, 31